UPPER ELEMENTARY LEVEL

CLASSICAL PIANO MASTERS

21 PIECES BY 17 COMPOSERS

ISBN 978-1-5400-8398-2

Copyright © 2020 by HAL LEONARD LLC
International Copyright Secured All Rights Reserved

Visit Hal Leonard Online at
www.halleonard.com

Contact us:
Hal Leonard
7777 West Bluemound Road
Milwaukee, WI 53213
Email: info@halleonard.com

In Europe, contact:
Hal Leonard Europe Limited
42 Wigmore Street
Marylebone, London, W1U 2RN
Email: info@halleonardeurope.com

In Australia, contact:
Hal Leonard Australia Pty. Ltd.
4 Lentara Court
Cheltenham, Victoria, 3192 Australia
Email: info@halleonard.com.au

CONTENTS

MUSETTE
from THE NOTEBOOK FOR ANNA MAGDALENA BACH, Appendix 126

Anonymous

ALLEGRETTO SCHERZANDO

CARL PHILLIP EMANUEL BACH
1714–1788

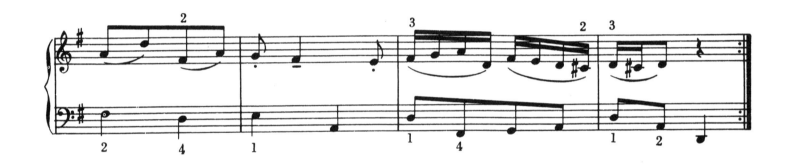

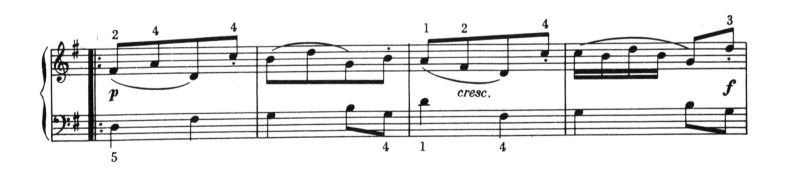

MARCH
from THE NOTEBOOK FOR ANNA MAGDALENA BACH, Appendix 122

CARL PHILIPP EMANUEL BACH
1714–1788

AIR

WILHELM FRIEDEMANN BACH
1710–1784

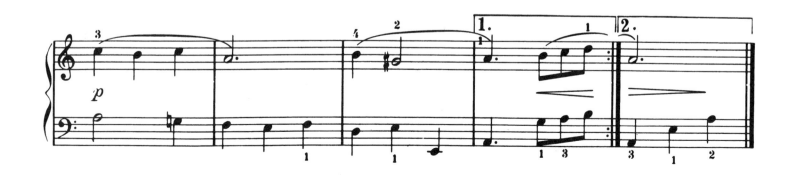

WALKING
from THE FIRST TERM AT THE PIANO, Sz. 53

BELÁ BARTÓK
(1881–1945)

Fingerings are by the composer.

ECOSSAISE IN G MAJOR

WoO 23

LUDWIG VAN BEETHOVEN
(1770–1827)

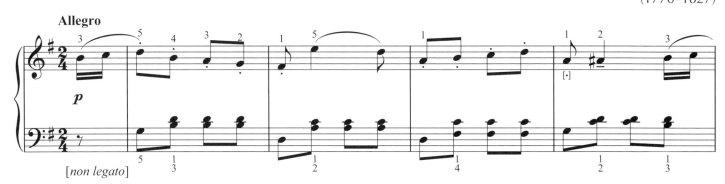

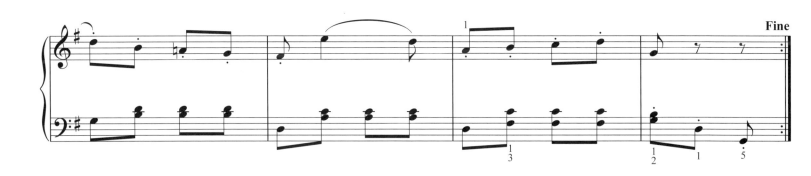

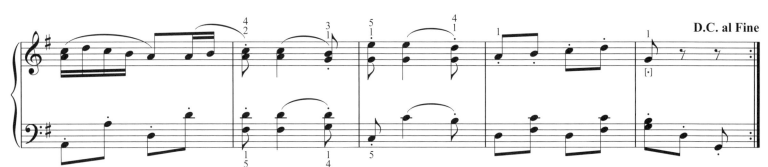

Fingerings are editorial suggestions.

MEOW! PURR!
from ALBUM FOR THE VERY YOUNG, Op. 103

MÉLANIE BONIS
(1858–1937)

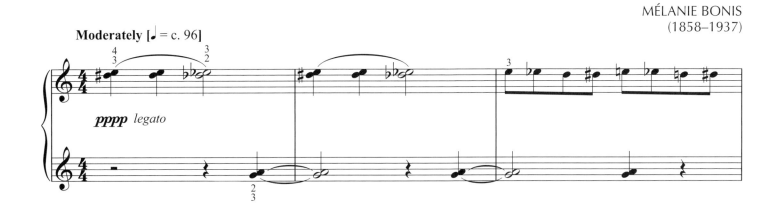

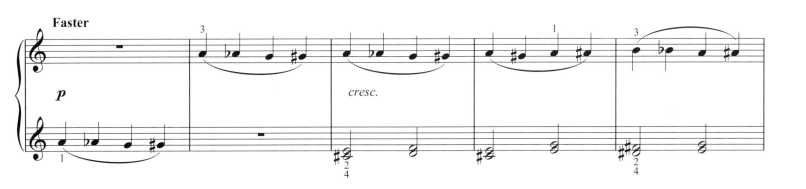

Fingerings are by the composer.

SONATINA IN C MAJOR
Op. 36, No. 1
First Movement

MUZIO CLEMENTI
1752–1832

With spirit

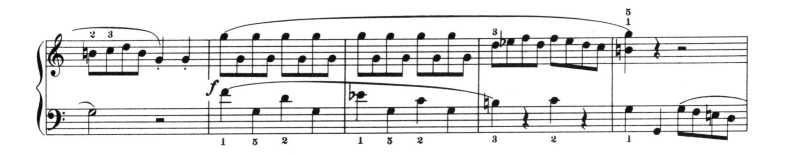

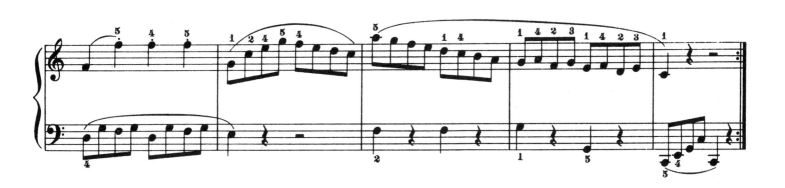

THE CHASE

WILLIAM DUNCOMBE
(ca. 1736–1818)

Fingerings, tempo, and dynamics are editorial suggestions.

TO SCHOOL
(Zur Schule)
from THE FIRST LESSONS, Op. 117, No. 14

CORNELIUS GURLITT
(1820–1901)

Fingerings are editorial suggestions.

CRADLE SONG
(Wiegenliedchen)
from THE FIRST LESSONS, Op. 117, No. 17

CORNELIUS GURLITT
(1820–1901)

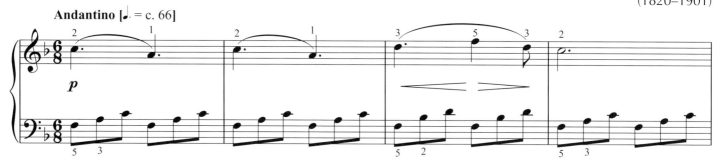

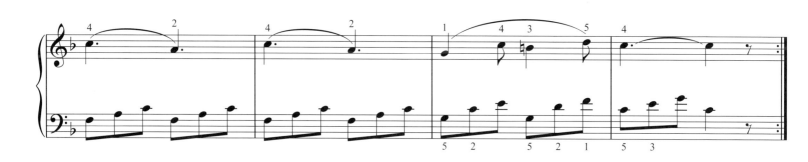

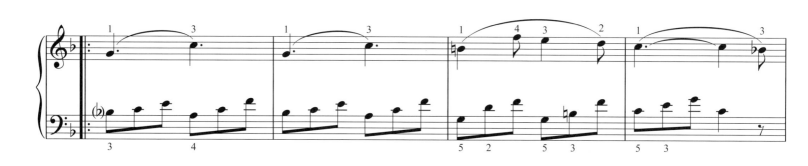

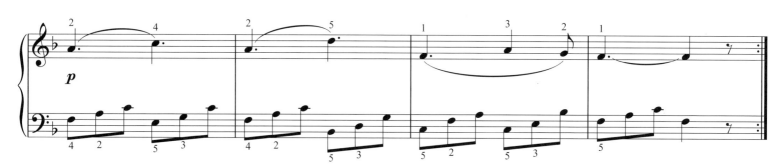

Fingerings are editorial suggestions.

BOURÉE IN G MINOR
"Impertinence"
HWV 494

GEORGE FRIDERIC HANDEL
1685–1759

GAVOTTE IN C MAJOR

GEORGE FRIDERIC HANDEL
1685–1759

MINUET IN C MAJOR

K. 6

WOLFGANG AMADEUS MOZART
(1756–1791)

[Andante moderato ♩ = ca. 100]

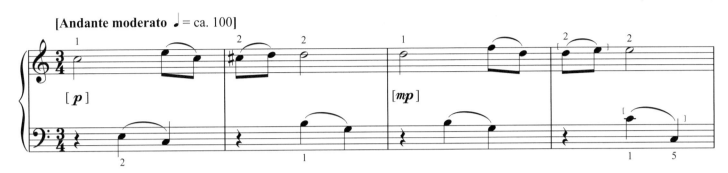

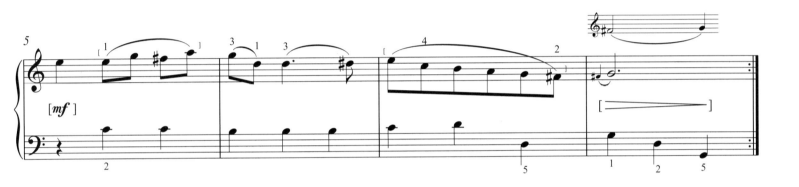

Fingerings are editorial suggestions.

MINUET IN B-FLAT MAJOR
K. 15pp

WOLFGANG AMADEUS MOZART
(1756–1791)

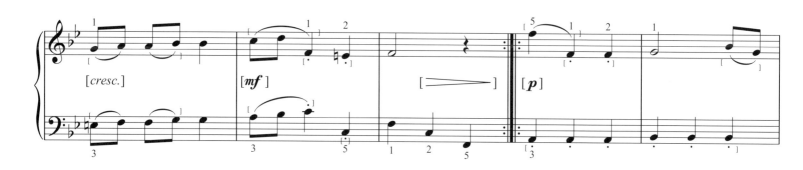

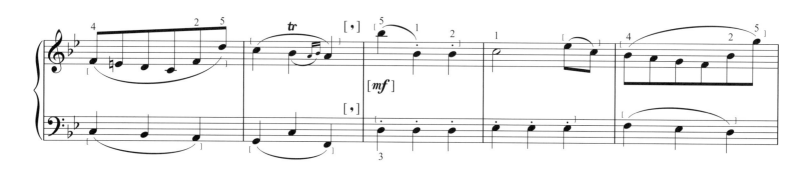

Fingerings are editorial suggestions.

THE CUCKOO

AUGUST EBERHARD MÜLLER
1767–1817

MINUET IN G MAJOR
from THE NOTEBOOK FOR ANNA MAGDELENA BACH, Appendix 114

CHRISTIAN PETZOLD
1677–1733

MINUET IN A MINOR
Z. 649

HENRY PURCELL
1659–1695

MENUET EN RONDEAU
(Minuet in the form of a Rondo)

JEAN-PHILIPPE RAMEAU
(1683–1764)

Play quarter notes slightly detached throughout.

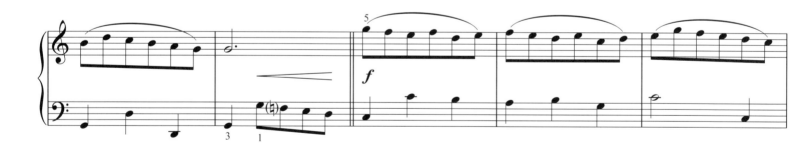

Dynamics, fingerings, and articulations are editorial suggestions.

MELODY
from ALBUM FOR THE YOUNG, Op. 68, No. 1

ROBERT SCHUMANN
1810–1856

Moderato

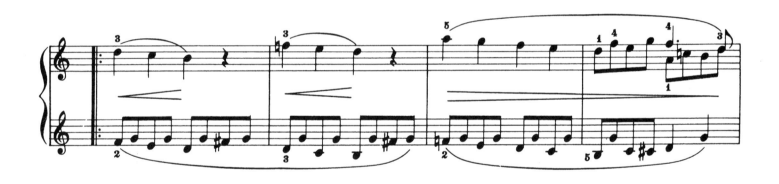

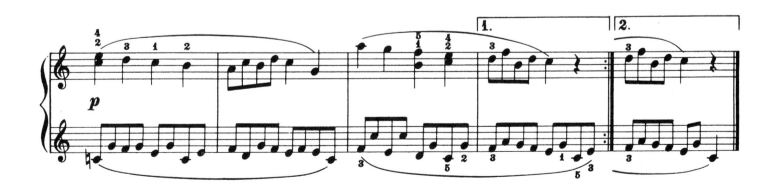

AMABILE
from SONATINA IN C MAJOR

CHARLES HENRY WILTON
(1761–1832)

Fingerings and articulations are editorial suggestions.